FELIZ NOCHEBUENA, FELIZ NAVIDAD

Christmas Feasts of
the Hispanic Caribbean

❧

MARICEL E. PRESILLA

pictures by

ISMAEL ESPINOSA FERRER

Henry Holt and Company · New York

To the memory of my uncle Oscar and my aunts Carolina,
Anita, Belén, Elena, and María Luisa for giving me
the gift of Christmas

For Chachi, Lindsay, Adrián, and Eric Martín, and for the
millions of Cuban children who have grown up without
Christmas memories

Henry Holt and Company, Inc. / *Publishers since 1866*
115 West 18th Street / New York, New York 10011
Henry Holt is a registered trademark of Henry Holt and Company, Inc.
Text copyright © 1994 by Maricel E. Presilla
Illustrations copyright © 1994 by Ismael Espinosa Ferrer
All rights reserved. Published in Canada by Fitzhenry & Whiteside Ltd..
195 Allstate Parkway, Markham, Ontario L3R 4T8.

Library of Congress Cataloging-in-Publication Data
Presilla, Maricel E.
Feliz Nochebuena, Feliz Navidad: Christmas feasts of the Hispanic
Caribbean / by Maricel E. Presilla ; pictures by Ismael Espinosa Ferrer.
1. Christmas—Caribbean Area—Juvenile literature.
2. Christmas cookery—Caribbean Area—Juvenile literature.
[1. Christmas—Caribbean Area.   2. Christmas cookery—Caribbean Area.]
I. Espinosa Ferrer, Ismael, ill.   II. Title.
GT4987.23.P74   1994   394.2'663'09729—dc20   93-43009
ISBN 0-8050-2512-X

First Edition—1994
The artist used watercolor and ink to create the illustrations for this book.
Printed in the United States of America on acid-free paper. ∞
1 3 5 7 9 10 8 6 4 2

As a child growing up on the crocodile-shaped island of Cuba, I could always tell that Christmas was coming by the blooming of my favorite mango tree. With the cool mist of December mornings also came ruby-red poinsettias and fields gleaming with the delicate pink and light-blue flowers of wild vines called *aguinaldos* (ah-ghee-*nahl*-dohs). Then, just in time for the holidays, clouds of silver fleece covered the wrought-iron fences of my grandfather's house with a white mantle.

In the narrow streets of Santiago de Cuba, my hometown, carts were heavy with piles of apples, pears, and grapes. Like special gifts, these imported holiday fruits came carefully wrapped in tissue-thin purple paper. Their colors and scents mixed with those of the winter fruits of my native island—*mameyes* (mah-*may*-yehs), sapodillas, sugar apples, tamarinds, soursops, oranges, and limes.

In the markets, crunchy Spanish nougats called *turrones* (too-*rroh*-nehs) competed for space with Cuban sweets. All of these candies, flowers, fruits, and vegetables announced the great Christmas feasts to come.

Many years ago, my family and I had to leave Cuba and move to Miami. Chachi, my first Cuban-American niece, knows it is Christmastime from the toys she sees in store windows, not from the flowers of our garden or the smells and colors of the local markets. But every December twenty-fourth as we gather in our tiny backyard in the shadow of Miami's skyscrapers, she hears my father tell the stories of Christmases past. He talks about a farm in the foothills of La Gran Piedra and feasts under the stars of the Caribbean sky.

And I tell her the story of the Christmas meals of the Hispanic islands, how they came to be, and all the people from around the world whose foods are on our table. It is an amazing story.

The Christmas celebrations enjoyed by the peoples of Cuba, Puerto Rico, and the Dominican Republic originated in Spain hundreds of years ago. In the time of Christopher Columbus, Spanish families gathered on Christmas Eve, *Nochebuena* (no-chay-*bway*-nah), to welcome the birth of Jesus with a quiet dinner. December twenty-fourth was a serious religious day, and most families ate a main dish of fresh or salt fish along with vegetables, special sweets, and *turrones*. After dinner, everyone went to church to hear *la misa de gallo* (la *mee*-sah day *gah*-yoh), or Mass of the Cockerel (Midnight Mass).

Unlike the simple Christmas Eve dinner, Christmas Day, or *Navidad* (nah-vee-*dahd*), was a day of great feasting. In palaces and castles, cooks prepared dozens of appetizing dishes, such as roast leg of fresh pork, tender suckling lamb or goat, capons and peacocks, and fresh or salt fish. While dining, guests were entertained by groups of carolers who sang happy Christmas songs called *villancicos* (vee-yahn-*see*-cohs).

Turrones and *mazapán* (mah-sah-*pahn*)—marzipan—were the most delicious of all the Spanish Christmas treats. Twelve hundred years ago, Muslims came to live in many parts of Spain. They were skilled farmers and they tended almond trees wherever they settled, even in the high mountains. They also planted fields of sugarcane along the blue Mediterranean coast of Alicante and Valencia and in the green fields of Andalusia. With these two simple ingredients, Muslim cooks prepared delicious candies that were eaten as snacks or at the end of long meals.

Over time, Muslims and Christians fought many battles for control of the land. By the middle of the thirteenth century, most of Spain had been conquered by Christian armies. But the tasty recipes of Muslim cooks were kept alive by Christian monasteries.

Columbus crossed the Atlantic in 1492, and at the end of his journey he found the most beautiful islands he had ever seen. The first Christmas Columbus and his sailors spent in the Caribbean, though, was very sad and gloomy. On Christmas Eve, they all stayed quietly aboard their ships probably eating salt fish and stale flour biscuits.

When his flagship capsized in the early morning of Christmas Day, Columbus was forced to land on the island of Hispaniola (now Haiti and the Dominican Republic).

The first festive meal Columbus was to have in the Christmas season of 1492 took place the next day on December twenty-sixth. The admiral was invited to a Taino chieftain's village to enjoy a native banquet. Instead of the familiar Spanish Christmas dishes, the Taino served spiny lobsters, three kinds of root vegetables, and *casabe* (cah-*sah*-bay)—a hard, round bread made with *yuca* (*yoo*-cah)—cassava.

Yuca is a tall shrub with thin, woody stems that produces long, swollen roots that are very good to eat. These roots were the most important food source of the Taino. To grow *yuca,* they prepared special mounded fields called *conucos* (coh-*noo*-cohs). Taino farmers, men and women, piled the earth high around cuttings from the stem of the *yuca* plant and waited from seven months to a year to harvest the thick, dark-skinned roots.

From *yuca,* the Taino prepared vinegar to season their meals and poison to coat their darts and arrows. They also boiled the peeled roots in a delicious soup called *ajiaco* (ah-hee-*ah*-coh) or grated them to make round, flat loaves of hearty *casabe.*

Of the gentle Taino of Hispaniola Columbus later wrote in his diary, "I believe that in all the world there is no better people nor better country." And he was right. While Columbus and his men were preparing to sail back to Spain, they enjoyed the generous Taino hospitality. With Taino help, the Spaniards also built a fort called Navidad—Christmas—in a part of Hispaniola that now belongs to Haiti, in remembrance of the day the *Santa María* sank.

This would have been the perfect ending for a Christmas story, but it is not the way things turned out. Columbus, and the Spaniards who followed him, eventually destroyed the Taino and their peaceful way of life.

In order to survive, Spaniards were forced to eat the native foods while waiting for the seeds and animals they had brought from Spain to bear fruit. To their disappointment, wheat, grape vines, and olive trees did not grow well in the hot, humid weather of the islands. But sugarcane and plantains brought from the Canary Islands thrived. Citrus trees grew green and luscious and were soon heavy with limes and bitter, rough-skinned Seville oranges. With citrus juice, the Spaniards made tasty marinades, *adobos* (ah-*doh*-bohs), and sauces called *mojos* (*mo*-hohs) to preserve their foods and to add zest to boiled *yuca,* the root vegetable that would become the favorite of the Cuban Christmas Eve table.

⚬✶⚬

The first pig brought by Columbus to Hispaniola left behind only one tooth, which has since been found by modern scientists. But the pigs that Columbus brought on his second voyage found the rugged island to their liking. They multiplied at an amazing rate and soon were everywhere. Pigs were also taken to other islands like Borinquén, which is now known as Puerto Rico.

Many escaped from their pigpens and became *cerdos jíbaros* (*sair*-dohs *hee*-bah-rohs), wild animals similar to the fierce boars of medieval Europe. They loved to forage in the dense forests of Hispaniola, and they hungrily ate their way through everybody's *conucos.*

Mojo Agrio

Garlic Sour Sauce for Boiled *Yuca*

The word *mojo* comes from the Spanish verb *mojar* (to wet). This savory sauce is used to wet, that is, to add flavor to, the Taino *yuca*. "Without *yuca* with *mojo*," said my grandfather Santiago, "there is no *Nochebuena*."

Makes 1 2/3 cups

12 cloves garlic, peeled
1 teaspoon salt or to taste
Pepper to taste
1/2 teaspoon cumin
1 cup Seville orange juice
(about 6 medium oranges) or a mix
of equal parts lime and orange juice
1/2 cup olive oil

Like most Caribbean sauces, *mojo agrio* (*mo*-hoh *ah*-gree-oh) can be prepared with mortar and pestle. Place garlic, salt, pepper, and cumin in the mortar and crush to a paste with the pestle. Add the citrus juice and olive oil and mix well. Spoon a tablespoon over piping hot *yuca* or other root vegetables, such as potatoes or yams.

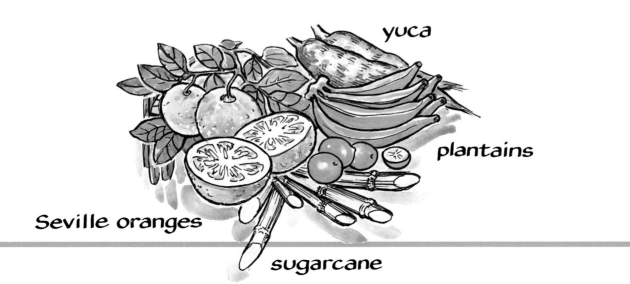

yuca

plantains

Seville oranges

sugarcane

In Cuba, where the eight pigs brought over by Diego Velázquez from the Canary Islands had grown to more than thirty thousand by 1514, the Spanish settlers organized colorful *monterías* (mawn-tay-ree-ahs), or hunting parties, that resembled those of medieval Spain. The men rode Andalusian horses and were accompanied by jumping, growling hunting dogs. Some pigs were salted on the spot to be turned into *tocino* (toh-*see*-noh)—bacon—or smoked to make *tasajo brujo* (tah-*sah*-hoh *broo*-hoh)—cured dried meat. Others were seasoned with an *adobo* made with the juice of Seville oranges. Then they were cooked on wooden grills or spit roasted over a fire often scented with the aroma of guava leaves, another trick the Spanish learned from the Taino. In time, spit roasting became the traditional way to cook a pig for the Christmas Eve dinner in all the Hispanic islands of the Caribbean.

Another group of people also added their foods and recipes to the Caribbean Christmas table. From the sixteenth century on, many Africans were brought to the islands to work as slaves on the sugarcane plantations. As in the rest of the Americas, they lived a hard, painful life. The Africans were given small parcels of land to cultivate native Caribbean plants, such as *yuca,* and some vegetables brought from Africa, such as plantains, *gandules* (gahn-*doo*-lehs)—green pigeon peas—and several varieties of a large, dark-skinned tuber called *ñame* (*nyah*-may)—yam. Plantation owners also gave them rations of salted beef and cod, as well as rice and beans. Although they never forgot their native foods and recipes, the Africans came to enjoy the new American foods, such as *yuca,* red kidney beans, and black beans.

Out of the kitchens of the African slaves on the great plantations came

several of my favorite Christmas dishes: boiled *ñame, congrí* (cohn-*gree*)—a mixture of rice and red kidney beans—and *Moros y Cristianos* (*moh*-rohs ee crees-tee-*ahn*-ohs). *Moros y Cristianos* (Moors and Christians), whose name recalls the people who once fought in Spain, is a tasty mix of white rice and black beans.

The cooking traditions of Spain and the many feasts of the Christian calendar flourished in Hispaniola, Cuba, and Puerto Rico. But the foods of the Christmas season changed through the centuries and from island to island. Native foods joined, and even replaced, Spanish Christmas favorites.

And just as the foods of Christmas changed, so did the day of true feasting. *Nochebuena,* the "good night," became the most important day of the Hispanic Caribbean Christmas season.

Little by little, as Spanish ships laden with provisions from Spain and the Canary Islands landed in the ports of the Caribbean islands, the colonists were able to purchase dried fruits, autumn and winter fruits, wooden boxes of *turrones* and sweet *mazapán* from Toledo, and apple cider from Asturias. With these new additions, the Caribbean Christmas table was set!

North Americans hope for a white Christmas. I dream of crystal clear, lightly cool Caribbean Christmas nights on a farm called Sevilla. There, in a house surrounded by lime trees, lived my uncle Oscar and my aunt Carolina. With them I spent some of the happiest days of my childhood. It was at Sevilla that I first learned to ride a horse and had my first taste of spit-roasted pork. At my aunt's table, all the foods and cooking traditions that had come together on my island through the centuries were shared by young and old alike on Christmas Eve.

From very early in the morning of December twenty-fourth, my aunt Carolina's kitchen was filled with busy women and excited children. There was much to be done: *yuca* and *ñame* to peel, bitter Seville oranges to squeeze to make *adobo* and *mojo,* plantains to fry, rice and beans to be cooked in large cast-iron cauldrons, and heaps of multicolored *turrones* to be cut into bite-size pieces. My uncle Oscar often came into the kitchen to mash more garlic and spices in a large mortar to add extra seasoning to the large pig that was hanging outside the kitchen waiting to be cooked.

As night fell, sparkling lightning bugs gathered around the clusters of flowers of a tall *mamoncillo* (mah-mawn-*see*-yoh) tree that grew near the farmhouse. My father would sit on the porch facing La Gran Piedra and name the Christmas stars.

While the women busily cooked food in the kitchen, the men of the family gathered around the smoldering pit where a large pig pierced by a stick of hardwood was rhythmically turned round and round to the sound of guitars. From time to time, my uncle Oscar would baste the pig with a garlicky Seville orange *adobo* to keep it juicy and tasty and add guava leaves to the fire. When it was all golden brown and ready to be taken out of the fire, the children would race to the pit to be the first to snatch the pig's crunchy tail.

Before long my aunt's table, covered with a starched linen tablecloth, bowed under the weight of the traditional foods of the Christmas season. My uncle Oscar carved the roasted pork. We also had *congrí*—the traditional rice dish of my hometown; *platanitos maduros* (pla-ta-*nee*-tohs mah-*doo*-rohs)—sweet, ripe fried plantains; and *tostones* (tos-*toh*-nehs)—green plantains fried golden. Large platters of boiled *yuca* and sliced *ñame* smothered in a tangy *mojo* sauce and *casabe*—my father's favorite bread—drizzled with olive oil rounded out the main course.

Generous helpings of all these foods were served on a single plate, accompanied by a refreshing salad of watercress, avocado, tomatoes, and radishes. We all drank ice-cold Asturian cider. It was sweet and delicious, and it tickled my nose every time I drank it.

For the children of the family, the end of the meal brought all the sweet, special treats I have told you about and more: *turrones; mazapán; nueces* (noo-*ay*-sehs)—walnuts; *avellanas* (ah-vay-*yah*-nahs)—hazelnuts; and slices of candied Seville orange served with *queso blanco* (*kay*-so *blahn*-coh)—a salty white cheese made with fresh cow's milk. People from western Cuba also ate *buñuelos* (boo-nyoo-*ay*-lohs), delicious figure-eight fritters made with *yuca* and yellow *malanga* (mah-*lahn*-gah) dough swimming in anise-flavored sugarcane syrup.

With our desserts we were allowed to take small sips of a potent homemade drink called *crema de vie* (*cray*-mah day *vyay*). All through the

Christmas season, guests at our house were offered tiny glasses of this very sweet but delicious eggnog. From time to time throughout the meal, we would stop eating and sing *villancicos*.

At midnight we toasted one another saying, "Feliz Nochebuena, Feliz Navidad—Merry Christmas Eve, Merry Christmas."

Back at Cuabitas, my grandfather's house, Christmas morning was always busy. Daybreak did not offer children the promise of toys. We had to wait until January 6 for these treats. But under our tree there was a beautiful *nacimiento* (nah-see-*myehn*-toh), a nativity scene with tiny figurines representing the birth of Jesus in Bethlehem. Our nativity was very Cuban. It showed the Holy Family in a *bohío* (bo-*ee*-oh), a Cuban farmer's hut surrounded by royal palms, and shepherds dressed like *guajiros* (gwah-*hee*-rohs)—Cuban farmers—offering gifts of plantains and *yuca* to baby Jesus. Each year we spent weeks helping my father make the lakes, hills, and huts.

Gathered around the *nacimiento,* my brother, my cousins, and I would sing our favorite *villancico,* one composed by my aunt Belén:

Unete cubano al coro
que entona el mundial clamor
ofrécele al pequeñito
tus palmares y tu son
Las flores que da tu suelo
tus ríos, playas, y sol
y el azul de nuestro cielo
que el mismito dibujó

Cuban, join the chorus
that all the people of the world sing,
offer the little one
your palm groves and your songs,
the flowers of your soil,
your rivers, beaches, and sun
the blue of our sky,
that He Himself has drawn

What I remember most of those early Christmas mornings at Cuabitas is the smell of delicious food. For breakfast, raisins, almonds, and olives were mixed with the leftovers of the Christmas Eve pork to prepare a tasty hash we called *montería*—a name that recalls the great pig hunts of earlier days. Outside in the backyard, my aunts Anita, Belén, Elena, and María Luisa took turns basting an enormous turkey that was cooked slowly in a big iron cauldron to be eaten for a late-afternoon Christmas lunch. Like many of the foods of the Cuban Christmas table, turkey came from a faraway land. When the Spaniards arrived in Cuba, there were no turkeys on the island. But in Mexico, Hernán Cortés and his soldiers found the large and colorful birds that had been domesticated by the Aztecs. The Aztecs cooked cut-up turkeys in earthenware casseroles with hot chile peppers.

Early in the sixteenth century, Spaniards took turkeys to Spain, where they were oven roasted whole, the way medieval cooks had once prepared peacocks. From Mexico, turkeys were brought to Cuba and the other Hispanic islands. In Cuba turkeys are called *pavos* (*pah*-vohs) or *guanajos* (gwan-*nah*-hohs), and they are marinated like the *Nochebuena* pork, with a delicious *adobo* made of lots of garlic, spices, and bitter Seville orange juice.

Adobo Tía Anita

Aunt Anita's *Adobo*

for Marinating a Large Turkey or Leg of Pork

Each Cuban family has secret tricks to make their food taste very special. This is my aunt Anita's recipe to marinate a large Christmas turkey or a large leg of pork. The secret is in the allspice, a very flavorful round and dark berry with the mixed scent of cinnamon and cloves that Columbus found in the Caribbean during his first voyage.

Makes 1 1/3 cups

> 6 Seville oranges, cut in half (or equal
> parts orange and lime juice)
> 1 head garlic
> 1 teaspoon allspice berries
> 1 teaspoon oregano
> 1 teaspoon cumin
> 1 bay leaf
> 1 teaspoon salt or to taste
> Pepper to taste

Equipment: Strainer, mortar and pestle

Children can help prepare the Christmas turkey by learning to make this tasty marinade with mortar and pestle. Squeeze the juice out of the Seville oranges. Strain the juice carefully to remove the bitter seeds and set aside. Peel the head of garlic and crush each clove lightly with the pestle to remove the skin. Place the garlic, allspice berries, oregano, cumin, bay leaf, salt, and pepper in the mortar and crush with the pestle until it becomes a mushy paste. Stir into the orange juice and mix well. With very clean hands, rub the *adobo* all over the turkey and inside its cavity and allow the bird to marinate overnight in the refrigerator. If marinating a leg of pork, rub the *adobo* all over it. Make sure to wash your hands thoroughly when you are done.

When my family and I left Cuba for the United States, two of my aunts, Josefina and Eve, and their children went to live in Puerto Rico. Puerto Rico is the third large island of the Greater Antilles Columbus visited on his second voyage. My family loves good food, music, and singing, and they soon found that Christmas in Puerto Rico was as joyous a season as it had once been in Cuba.

As *Nochebuena* approaches, groups of carolers visit friends and neighbors and ask for *aguinaldos* (gifts) as well as food and drink. Some arrive playing traditional musical instruments like the *güiro* (*gwee*-roh)—a percussion instrument made with a gourd—the *cuatro* (*quah*-troh)—a four-stringed guitar—and *maracas* (mah-*rah*-kahs)—hand-held instruments made of dried gourds. Since these singing groups always come without warning, their visits are called *asaltos* (ah-*sahl*-tohs)—assaults. The carolers must be invited in and offered food and creamy *coquito* (coh-*kee*-toh), a traditional Christmas drink made with coconut milk and rum. Otherwise, they make a lot of noise.

When Puerto Rico was still a colony of Spain, groups of carolers singing *villancicos* were called *trullas* (*troo*-yahs). Those who are old enough to remember say that the best *trullas* were those of the Puerto Rican countryside. All through the Christmas season, and especially on the eve of the Three Kings Feast on January sixth, rich and poor farmers went up and down the hills and deep into the woods to visit friends and relatives and surprise them with their songs:

De la montaña venimos	We come from the mountain
para invitarte a comer	to invite you to eat
un lechoncito en su vara	a small pig roasted on the spit
y ron pitorro a beber	and homemade rum to drink

The wealthy people went on horseback, and the poorer ones on foot. But they were all welcomed with delicious foods and drinks. After dining, everyone sang and danced.

Coquito
Creamy Coconut Drink

Although this rich coconut drink is traditionally made with white rum, my Puerto Rican cousin Elbita prepares a creamy and frothy nonalcoholic *coquito* that is also delicious. The best *coquitos* are made with fresh coconut milk, but you can also use canned.

Makes 5 cups

1 12-ounce can evaporated milk
1 14-ounce can condensed milk
2 egg yolks*
1 15-ounce can coconut milk or
1 cup fresh coconut milk (see recipe)
Pinch of salt
1/4 teaspoon ground cinnamon

Place all the ingredients in a blender and process for 3 minutes at high speed. Store in a glass bottle in the refrigerator and serve when it is thoroughly cool.

To make your own fresh coconut milk, grate the meat from 2 medium coconuts with a grater. Place in a bowl and add 1 1/2 cups warm water. Allow to rest for five minutes. Strain the liquid. Place the remaining pulp in a cheesecloth and make a bundle. Squeeze tight to extract more coconut milk. Set aside until ready to make *coquito*.

*If concerned about salmonella, omit the raw eggs from the recipe. You can use pasteurized egg blends sold in supermarkets instead.

As in Cuba and the Dominican Republic, spit-roasted pork or *puerco en vara* (poo-*air*-coh ehn *vah*-rah) is the centerpiece of the Puerto Rican Christmas Eve table. But the Christmas feast could never be complete without *pasteles* (pahs-*tay*-lehs), a tasty steamed package of grated tropical vegetables and tubers wrapped in plantain leaves, everyone's favorite treat.

To make *pasteles* in large quantities is time-consuming, and the women of the family get together early in December to prepare them by the hundred. To start, plantains, green bananas, and *yautía* (yah-oo-*tee*-ah) together, or *yuca* by itself, are peeled and grated to a paste to make a dough. Then the women prepare a tasty *sofrito* (soh-*free*-toh) to add flavor to the dough. The Puerto Rican *sofrito* is a savory mix of garlic, onions, Italian frying peppers, *ají dulce* (ah-*hee dool*-say)—a tiny lantern-shaped pepper—a perfumed herb called *cilantrillo* (see-lahn-*tree*-yoh) —coriander—tomato paste, and diced fresh pork.

The *pastel* dough is given a bright orange-yellow color with an oil tinted with *achiote* (ah-chee-*oh*-tay), **pasteles** the seeds of a plant used by the Taino Indians to color their bodies and their food. The women carefully place spoonfuls of dough on a square of parchment paper or on a plantain leaf. A little bit of the *sofrito* is placed in the center of the dough. Then the edges of the plantain leaf or paper are carefully folded over the dough to form a small rectangular package. This is tied with a string and later steamed. The plantain leaves give the *pasteles* a very special flavor.

yuca

plantains

yautía

ají dulce

peppers

coriander

The happiest day of the Christmas season in Puerto Rico is the *Fiesta de Reyes* (fee-*ehs*-tah day *ray*-ehs)—Three Kings Feast—the Day of the Epiphany. According to Christian tradition, three wise men from the Orient—Gaspar, Melchior, and Balthasar—followed the star of Bethlehem to bring baby Jesus precious gifts of gold, myrrh, and frankincense.

The Three Kings, or *Los Tres Reyes Magos* (lohs trehs *ray*-ehs *mah*-gohs), are beloved figures in the three Hispanic islands. There was a time in Puerto Rico when Christmas trees were not yet popular, and people decorated their homes with beautiful wooden statues of the Three Kings. These images were hand carved and carefully painted in bright colors by artisans called *santeros* (sahn-*tay*-rohs), or image makers.

Each child has a favorite king—Gaspar, Melchior, or Balthasar—to whom he or she writes letters asking for gifts, just as American children do with Santa Claus. On the eve of the Three Kings Feast, children place containers of grass under their beds for the three kings' camels. By early morning the grass is gone and children instead find dozens of treats and toys under the tree. The presents the kings bring to the baby Jesus are a reminder of all the peoples—Arabs, Taino, Spaniards, and Africans—who have brought their food to our Hispanic Christmas feasts. And now that many Hispanic people have come to live in the United States, our foods and flavors are our gifts to the American Christmas table.

Glossary

Unfamiliar words are defined on first use. Here are additional information and references for frequently used terms.

achiote: The orange seeds of a tropical American bush that add a beautiful yellow color and a delicate nutty flavor to food.

adobo: The Old Spanish word *adobo* came from the French *adober,* to dub a knight with his weapons: sword and spurs. When referring to cooking, *adobar* means to flavor and ennoble food.

aguinaldos: In Cuba, these are Christmas songs as well as the name of a winter flower; in other parts of the Hispanic Caribbean, these are Christmas gifts.

casabe: A flat, unleavened *yuca* bread made by the Taino.

cassava: A native American root vegetable with a coarse brown skin and milky white flesh.

conucos: Mounded fields where the Taino Indians cultivated root vegetables such as *yuca.*

malanga: Cuban name given to a dark-skinned native American root vegetable with a starchy white or yellow flesh. Puerto Ricans use the word *malanga* to refer to taro, another root vegetable of Asian origin.

mamey: A fruit native to the Caribbean and Central America. It is shaped like a small football with brown skin that feels like sandpaper. Its sweet salmon-colored flesh encloses a large, shiny black seed.

mamoncillo: Quenep, a tall tropical American tree that bears round, small, and green fruits that grow in clusters like grapes. The hard skin encloses a large round seed enveloped by a delicious salmon-colored pulp. Children eat the pulp of the *mamoncillo* and then use the round seeds as marbles.

ñame: True yam, a root vegetable native of several tropical regions of the world. Some varieties are tiny, but others can grow as large as a man's leg.

Navidad: Christmas.

Nochebuena: Christmas Eve.

plantains: Large bananas used in cooking. They were brought to Hispaniola from the Canary Islands by the Spaniards in 1516.

sapodillas: Small round American fruits with brown skin and sweet granular pulp. In Cuba, they are called *nísperos.*

soursops: *Guanábanas,* large heart-shaped fruits native to tropical America. They have a thick green skin speckled with small soft spines and a cottony sweet-and-sour pulp with tiny black seeds.

sugar apples: *Anones,* heart-shaped green fruits covered with thick scales. They have a custardlike white granular pulp.

Taino: Arawak Indians of South American origin who inhabited the islands of Cuba, Hispaniola, and Puerto Rico at the time of the Spanish conquest.

tamarinds: *Tamarindos,* the tart pods of the tamarind tree, an evergreen plant of East African origin grown in all of Latin America and even in Florida. When mature, the fruits turn into brown pods with a tart but very pleasant pulp.

turrones: Spanish Christmas sweets made with crushed almonds and honey or sugar.

villancico: Christmas carol. Also called *aguinaldos* in Cuba and Puerto Rico.

yautía: Taino word used in Puerto Rico for the root vegetable Cubans call *malanga.*

yuca: See cassava.

Bibliography

Quotes from the diary of Columbus were drawn from Samuel Eliot Morison, trans., *Journals and Other Documents on the Life and Voyages of Christopher Columbus* (New York: The Heritage Press, 1963). References to archaeological findings in the site of Columbus's colony of La Navidad were drawn from the accounts of the expedition led by the Florida State Museum; see Kathleen A. Deagan, "Searching for Columbus's Lost Colony" (*National Geographic,* vol. 172, No. 5 [November 1987], 672–75). According to the zooarchaeologists of the Florida State Museum, a pig's tooth found in the well of La Navidad belonged to a European animal that grew near Seville in Spain. They believe this pig was brought to the island of Hispaniola aboard the *Santa María.* Information about pre-Columbian and colonial Cuban history were primarily drawn from the Spanish-language multivolume work of Levi Marrero; see Levi Marrero, *Cuba, Economía y Sociedad* (Madrid: Editorial Playor, 1978). For a lively description of Puerto Rican *trullas,* see Manuel A. Alonso, *El jíbaro* (Puerto Rico: Cultural Puertorriqueña, 1986).